Illustrations of Geometric Tracery, from the Paneling Belonging to Carlisle Cathedral

Robert William Billings

O. Tyndall Bruce, Esq
Falkland House
Falkland

Drawn by R.W.Billings. Engraved by John Sadler

SCREEN OF S.T CATHERINES CHAPEL.

London, Published by I.Virtue, ... N.º 26 Ivy Lane E.C.

ILLUSTRATIONS

OF

GEOMETRIC TRACERY,

FROM THE PANELING BELONGING TO

Carlisle Cathedral.

BY

ROBERT WILLIAM BILLINGS,

AUTHOR OF THE ILLUSTRATIONS AND HISTORY OF CARLISLE CATHEDRAL.

London:

PUBLISHED BY THOMAS AND WILLIAM BOONE, 29, NEW BOND STREET;

AND THE AUTHOR, MANOR HOUSE, KENTISH TOWN.

1842.

The second view of the Screen is from the Author's Illustrations of Carlisle Cathedral. It has been thought advisable to reprint it here for the better explanation of the subject to those who are not in possession of that work.

R. W. B.

ILLUSTRATIONS,

THE Geometric Panels forming the present Illustrations are the remains of an exceedingly valuable and extensive collection, for the whole Choir of Carlisle Cathedral, eastward of the still beautiful stalls, was separated from the aisles by Screens filled with elaborate Tracery. The same enrichment extended also to the Chapel of St. Catherine, a small building, which may be termed an aisle to the south transept.

In the year 1764, the Cathedral was, according to the Churchwardens' usual phrase, repaired and "*beautified*." The whole of the Choir screens were removed, and their place occupied by a high stone wall, covered in the Choir by a wooden arcade in the true Gothic style of that period, and in the aisles by a carefully-executed coat of plaister. The old and useless paneling was removed to some of the outbuildings, and by far the greater portion either lost or destroyed.

All that remains of the original enrichments may be described as the frame-work of an exceedingly mutilated screen, in the possession of William Cowper, Esq. at Carlton Hall, near Penrith, from which is derived the materials for Plates XIX. and XX., and three of the borders in Plate XVIII.; three beautiful Panels (Plates XV. XVI. XVII.) forming part of a sideboard at Featherstone Castle, Northumberland, the seat of Lord Wallis (formerly proprietor of Carlton Hall); one Panel (Plate VIII.), and the fourth border of Plate XVIII. inserted in the modern doorway to the aisle of the Choir against the Bishop's Throne.

Fortunately, the Chapel of St. Catherine was not considered worth *beautifying*, and in this building we have two screens, containing the remainder of the subjects represented, numbering thirteen out of twenty. Three or four Panels at present in the Chapel belonged to the Choir. The originals, most probably, from being more beautiful, were cut away; the ends of the original tracery being still left, give very much the appearance of their having been taken to fit a particular piece of furniture.

The whole of these screens are reputed to be the work of Prior Thomas Gondibour, who presided over the Cathedral from 1484 to 1507. His initials (𝕿. 𝕲.) were beautifully cut in the Tracery of a Panel in the doorway shewn in the frontispiece, but this was unfortunately pulled out and taken away by some mischievous person in the winter of 1839. Another cypher (T. G.) forming the cusps of a trefoil from Carlisle (see Plate XX.) may be taken for Prior Gondibour's. It is among the remains at Carlton Hall. Their date may therefore fairly be taken at about 1500.

Some of these specimens are perhaps not so interesting in themselves for elegance of design, as from the circumstance of their proving that the majority were designed on the same ground-work, namely, the division of a square into four parts each way, or sixteen squares. Upon the lines of these squares the centres of all the curves are worked, and upon such a simple calculation of parts, as to render their construction perfectly easy. It is of essential importance to have a ready means, well known, of re-producing the beautiful forms displayed in many of these and other specimens, and the author trusts that the means he has adopted will effect this, for no workman, following the descriptions given of each Plate, can possibly err in any of the leading features.

From the direct evidence here produced of system in the minor detail of a once beautiful church, is it not fair to assume that the mis-called *Gothic* Architects had a system for objects of greater magnitude, that is the buildings themselves?

In the leading curves of these examples, nothing can exceed their accuracy of projection, but all the foils contained within are (most probably from their diminutive size) worked by hand. In fact, they are too small to be otherwise, unless the most extraordinary fastidiousness had been exercised upon them.　They are all drawn half the real size, except Plates IX. and X. which are the full dimensions.

The two screens, as shewn in the frontispiece, and in the Plate from the author's work on Carlisle Cathedral, may be briefly described as consisting of a basement of draped Panels, and immediately above them a series of perforated Geometric Panels.　Above these is a plain string, surmounted in the former Plate by a series of smaller Panels, and in the latter by the running border shewn in Plate XI.　The upper portion of the screen is a series of detached piers, all ornamented in one screen by flying buttresses, and in the other a buttress on each alternate pier.　Above the buttresses is a square-headed capital, and the space between this and the upper string (ornamented alternately over each pier with a head and leaves) is filled with tracery, the cusps of the lower arch being ornamented with leaves.

The string is surmounted by a richly decorated parapet, with a border of leaves connected at the top by a bead.　In the centre of each parapet is a shield, the armorial bearings of which have disappeared.　The whole of the frame-work of the mutilated screen at Carlton Hall was ornamented with the bordering, shewn in Plate XVIII. fig. B.

DESCRIPTION OF THE PLATES.

Plate II. The specimen at the side of this Plate is the simplest as regards the division of the Panel into sixteen squares, consisting in fact of sixteen equal quatrefoils. The construction of Plate II. is equally simple, being composed of the arc of a circle, whose boundary touches the points *b*, *c*, *d*, the centre *a*. being determined by the intersection of lines perpendicular to the chords *b. c.* and *b. d.* The trefoil is composed of equal circles within the triangle *e*.

Plates III. IV. V. The centres of the principal figure in these examples will be found at the angles and centre of the parallelogram, containing two equilateral triangles, as marked on the margin of Plate III. (*a*)

Plate III. Draw the circle A. and arcs A. A, and within it the two circles B. The triangular spaces left within the figure are filled with the circles C. The upper and lower extremities have semi-quatrefoils. The circle filling the space which should correspond with C. is larger on account of the Panel being made square instead of the parallelogram of a hexagon, whereby the additional space shewn in the small diagram *(b)* is added to the figure.

Plate IV. This is varied by changing the two inner circles, *b c.* from the width to the length of the figure. The radius of the small circle *d.* is one third of the largest, as figured. This example is rather less in height than width: the inequality mentioned in the last is consequently less apparent.

Plate V. The difference of this example, from the preceding, is in the small circle (E.) being brought to the centre of the principal figure, instead of the extremity, and in the introduction of another circle (D.) into the triangular space, between the circles, A. B. C.

Plate VI. This is also a variation of the preceding example, but the divisions of the height and width, approach nearer to a square, the parallelogram of the Panel being nearly in the proportion of $\frac{22}{21}$. Produce the semicircle A. of one half the width of the Panel, and the segments B. from the centre *a*, intersecting the points, *b. c.*

Plate VII. The arrangement of this beautiful example, differs totally from the preceding, and the division of height and width are perfectly equal. Divide the square into four parts, and from figure 3 of these produce the circle *a*. The distance between the boundary of this circle and the intersection of the square, at *b*, gives the radius of the small circle c. These circles being produced at the intersection of the alternate squares, the outer connecting arc (*d*.) is struck from the point *g*, touching the small circles at *e. e.* and the intersection of the square at *f*.

Plate VIII. This is perfectly square, and divided in the same manner as the preceding examples. The diagonals of each square being drawn, produce the circle A, within four of the diagonal squares. The small circle B, of two-thirds the diameter of the preceding, completes the outline.

Plate IX. The sub-division into small squares is here dispensed with, but the whole subject is a repetition of each figure four times. Draw the diagonals of the square, and from the angle of the Panel draw the quadrant A, and within it the circle B, touching *a*, *b*, *c*. Divide the radius of A into three parts; the diagonal of the first gives the radius of the smaller circle c. Within the quadrants the space is filled by four equal circles D.

Plates X. and XI. are small examples, above the larger Panels in the view of the Screen. These have been terminated by an enrichment of leaves, a portion of which is still left.

Plate X. Draw the diagonals A. A, and within them the semicircle B. from the centre *a*, on the smaller side of the parallelogram. The semicircles c are from *b b*, on the longer side. The semicircle D. is a repetition of this.

Plate XI. Draw the semicircles A. A; and from *a*. produce that marked B. The radius of c. is one-sixth the length of the Panel, and that of D. one-third the width. E. is from the figure *b*, touching the line D. at c.

The border in this Plate belongs to the Screen in the aisle of the Choir. The leading lines are only repetitions of the tracery described on Plate V.

Plate XII. *Archway of the Screen*—Draw the semicircle A. from *a*, and divide its radius into 11 parts. From figure 6, produce the quadrant J, and from *b*. the semicircle K. Draw a line from the centre *a*. through the angle B. The point D, equal in distance from it as B, c, is the centre of the curve E. F. is a repetition of this upon the line G. The smaller curve H, is portion of a semicircle touching F and c, its centre being on the boundary line of the Panel. The upper portion of the curve is a repetition of this from the point *c*. *e* is a quadrant from the centre *a*, and the lower part or continuation *f*, is from the centre (*d*), upon a line drawn from *a*, through the 12th part of the scale before named.

Plate XIII. is a large Panel upside down in the view of the Screen. This specimen did not originally belong to it, and has been placed there to fill up a gap, occasioned by the destruction of the original work. It is represented at *a*, the remainder of the Plate being a portion half the full size.

Plate XIV. *The Parapet.* The great semicircle forming the leading line of the figure is the same as described in the border of Plate XI., and the remainder of the tracery is very nearly the same as in Plate V. The outline of the border-leaf is the diagonal of a square.

Plate XV. is a repetition of the same circle, whose centre is the intersection of each division or square.—Produce the circle A. from the centre *a*, and corresponding circles from *b* and *c*; their intersection cuts off 1-6th from each side of A, marked B and c, and represented by the dotted line.

Plate XVI. Divide the panel into four portions, and draw the diagonals A. A. Within each triangle strike the circle B; and in the angles of the square the small circles c. c. The arc D is a portion of the first circle.

Plate XVII. Draw the diagonals of the square, as A. A. Within the triangle draw the circle B, and within this the four smaller circles c, the parts represented by the dotted lines being left out in the complete figure. Draw the circle in the angles of the square (D.) The limit of the circle E. is determined by a perpendicular, *a.* dropped from the centre of the circle B.

Plate XVIII.—*Borders.* Figure A. is in the doorway of the Choir against the Bishop's Throne. . This elegant little specimen is the repetition of semicircles whose radius is one half, and one quarter the width of the border; the ground-work being precisely the same as the majority of the Panels—namely, four squares each way.

Fig. B. is peculiar for the leafy border on each side.

Fig. c. is the same as the subject of Plate XV. And

Fig. D. very strongly resembles the Tracery of Plate V.

Plates XIX. and XX. All that remains of these Panels is the framework and ends of the tracery.—No. XIX. has sufficient to identify the design, but No. XX. is not to be depended on for originality. They are both peculiar from the sub-division of the Panel into four distinct parts, by the diagonal rib of Plate XIX., and the cross-rib with the angles rounded off in Plate XX.

THE END.

G. NORMAN, PRINTER, MAIDEN LANE, COVENT GARDEN.

Drawn by R.W.Billings.

Etched by G.B.Smith.

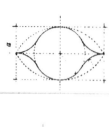

Drawn by R. W. Billings

Etched by R. B. Smith

London Published by J. Weale & R. W. Billings December 1842

Drawn by H W Rollidaye.   Etched by H Smith.

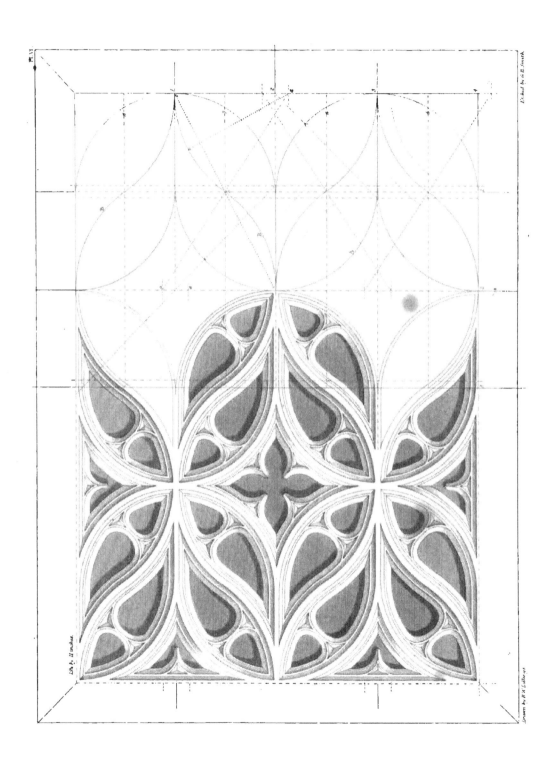

Drawn by R.K. Gilbert.

Etched by G.B. Smith.

Pl. VII

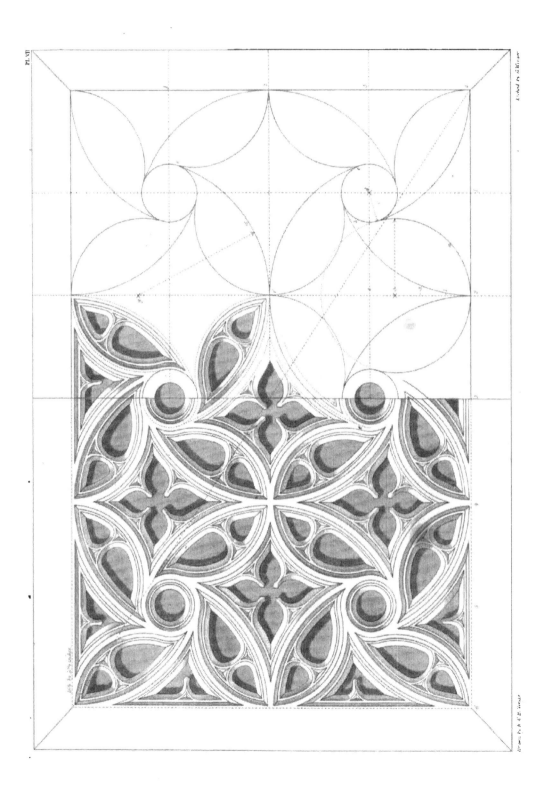

Printed by G Weiss.

Drawn by H W Billings
Etched by G B Sma
GOTHIC PAVEMENT OF PECOLATE & GEOMETRIC TILES

Plate IX Full size

Plate X full size

Drawn by R W Billings

Etched by J B Smith

GOTHIC TRACERIES OF CARLISLE CATHEDRAL.

GROINING LANCELOT'S OR CRANMER'S CANTERBURY.

Drawn by F. M. Dobbins.

Etched by G. B. Smith.

London, Published by T. & W. Boone, & R. W. Billings, December 1842.

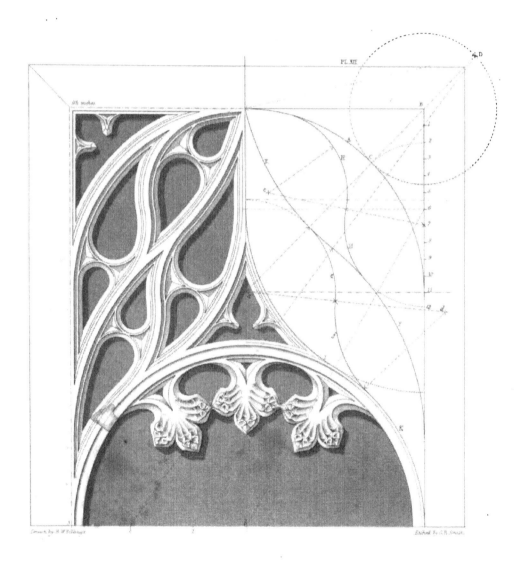

London Published by T & W Boone & R & Billings December 1 1842.

Drawn by R W B Binns

Etched by G B Smith

Drawn by P.W. Pilkins.

Etched by G.R. Smith.

Pl. XVI

Drawn by R.W.Billings.

Etched by G.Winter.

Drawn by R W Billings

GOTHIC PANELLING OF THE XVTH CENTURY

Etched by J B Smith.

London, Published by T & A Barne & R H Billings December 11 1843

Drawn by R. W. Billings.

Etched by G. B. Smith.

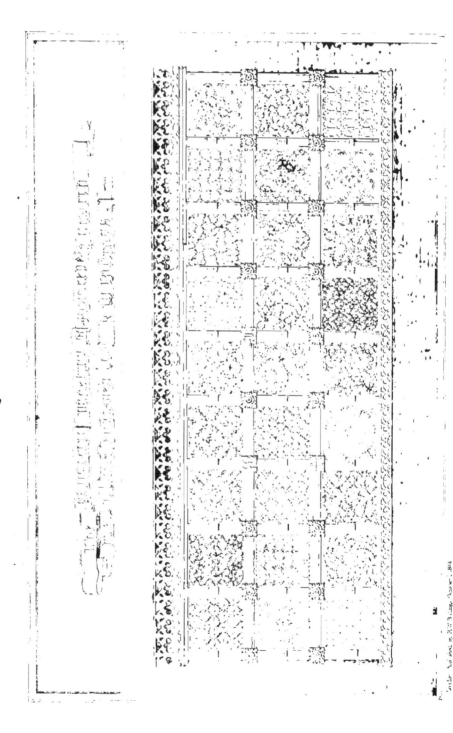

THE

GEOMETRIC TRACERY

OF

BRANCEPETH CHURCH,

IN THE

COUNTY OF DURHAM.

ILLUSTRATED BY

ROBERT WILLIAM BILLINGS.

LONDON:
PUBLISHED FOR THE AUTHOR, BY
THOMAS AND WILLIAM BOONE, 29, NEW BOND-STREET;
AND BY
GEORGE ANDREWS, SADDLER-STREET, DURHAM.
1845.

INTRODUCTORY ACCOUNT

OF

THE BRANCEPETH PANELS.

The title plate furnishes a complete miniature resemblance of the whole subject set forth in the following illustrations. It would perhaps be difficult to find in any similar production of art so many designs represented in so small a compass, and at the same time exhibiting memorials of Gothic skill so full of interest, although produced at comparatively a late period, viz., about the year 1500. Various conjectures might easily be formed as to the original use to which the mass of ornament here delineated was applied, but according to tradition the prototype belonged to the ancient Rood Screen of Brancepeth Church, and was removed to the place it now occupies over the chancel arch at the time of the erection of the present Screen by Bishop Cosin,[1] who was previously Rector of Brancepeth.

It has undoubtedly been a portion of the crowning member of a screen or a monument, because the three divisions are slightly canted (canopy like) and surmounted by a foliated border.

At each end of the paneling, corresponding fragments are clearly discernible, giving undeniable evidence that the magnitude of the original work exceeded its present dimensions. It may, however, be considered fortunate that so much practical knowledge relating to tracery has been bequeathed to us in the construction of these remarkable specimens, and although some are marred by singularity rather than distinguished by beauty, they form in the aggregate a most interesting collection, as they bear in a remarkable manner upon the system of

---

[1] Bishop of Durham (1660-1672.)

construction employed in the geometric paneling in Carlisle Cathedral, which has been completely illustrated by the author of the present volume.

Possibly we are indebted to the genius of the same individual for the analogous designs of which the Church of Brancepeth and the Cathedral just named are the depositories, or, if they are not the results of one master-mind, they must undoubtedly be ascribed to individuals guided by the same rules of art. Upon comparison of the histories of Carlisle and Durham, arguments are adducible that the former conjecture is a true one, because two distinguished persons respectively connected with each place must have been brought into intimate association by their ecclesiastical position,—we mean the reputed author of the Carlisle tracery, Thomas Gondibour, Prior of Carlisle (1484-1507), and Richard Bell, Prior of Durham, who was Bishop of Carlisle from 1478 to 1496; and our conjecture is greatly strengthened by the fact, that most of the works, if not all, in the churches of the diocese of Durham emanated from the dignitaries of the Cathedral establishment in that city. Hexham Abbey, in Northumberland, equidistant between Carlisle and Brancepeth, contains in its organ screen some tracery which forms a remarkable connecting link between the same class of ornament in both places, and was almost to a certainty designed by the same hand.

But the greatest proof of the relationship of these compositions is their geometric foundation,—thus each series commences with a simple elementary panel composed of a number of quatrefoils within an equal number of squares. Proceeding from that primitive form, the centres of the curves being upon the same foundation lines, the designs become so complicated that it is by no means easy to decipher their construction, and some indeed, without close investigation, might, by the complexity of their apparently fanciful intersections, be said to have refused subjection to the regularity of linear projection, and consequently might be placed among those produced in modern times by "rule of thumb."

With their similarity in construction and size, for the paneling in both edifices is as nearly as possible of the same dimensions, all comparison ends. Thus that at Carlisle is pierced, and each panel is displayed separately, between the piers of a screen, while the tracery of Brancepeth (sunk only to the depth of a quarter of an inch) is a mass of design merely divided by small ribs. Another remarkable difference results from the form of the mouldings, for the leading curves of the Carlisle specimens are well defined by an upper moulding or bead *a* and the minor tracery of trefoils and quatrefoils upon a lower moulding *b* (*see Plate* 15, *fig*. A).

Here the Brancepeth panels suffer by comparison, for both the leading lines and the minor tracery are upon one moulding (*see* B, *Pl*. 15), and there is consequently an appearance of confusion and indecision in the whole composition. To make up, however, for this defect, the ornament as well as a portion of the ground is richly gilded, and the remainder of the ground coloured in the manner of this specimen.

The partial gilding of the ground is probably unique, and it certainly gives an air of substance to the tracery, which is characterised by tenuity, and is too shallow in depth to be effective. But gilding and painting have not saved them from decay, for the corrosions of the worm and the despoiling agency of time are fast working the destruction of these reliques of antiquity.

The specimens of this collection are drawn one-third of the actual size, excepting Plates 1 and 2, which are one-fourth. The height of the panels slightly exceeds their width, but this disproportion does not mar the general design of the tracery, the framework of which is supposed to be a perfect square, and, generally speaking, the additional height contains portions of a repetition of the pattern.

Throughout the diagrams, the circles used in the formation of the designs are marked out by dotted curves, which in all cases are omitted in the complete pattern. We have refrained from entering into very minute details of the various lines which form a key to each pattern, because the plate itself, in all the minor points, furnishes at once to the eye a complete linear solution, and our intended limits would have been far exceeded had we entered into lengthy descriptions of those parts which the graphic exposition itself renders obvious.

The comparatively recent date of the specimens now before us, and perhaps certain questionable peculiarities or anomalies discoverable in their style, may be liable to objection. Their real value, however, consists in the beautiful illustration of principle which they develope, and on this account they are certainly deserving of the most attentive consideration.

It is satisfactory to find that the more we examine Gothic architecture, the more we are convinced that chance was in no possible way connected with the linear designs of construction. The most exuberant richness of contour can, by a careful analysis, be reduced to simple geometric rules; and in the investigation of the laws of description which we have here endeavoured to exhibit, it has been curious to observe how extraordinary an alteration in the general features of such panels as have fallen under our notice is affected by a very slight deviation in that most simple of all curves—the arc of a circle.

There are several distinct geometric species in the panels under notice; these are—

1. Those composed of circles or their arcs, having all their centres upon the sides of a given number of squares or their diagonals. This class comprises the Plates figured respectively 3 to 10 inclusive, numbers 1 and 2 on Plate 1, number 1 on Plate 2, and numbers 3 and 4 on Plate 12. In some cases the sides of these squares and their diagonals, especially the latter, form a decided and positive portion of the pattern (see Plate 1, No. 2, and Plates 3 and 6).

2. Where the principal frame work is a series of circles of equal radius touching each other, three of whose centres are consequently at the angular points of an equilateral triangle (see figure A, Plate 1). The continuous curve·produced by the arcs between the points of tangency of these circles in mutual contact is known by the term "ogee." Numbers 3 and 4 on Plate 1, No. 3 on Plate 2, and Plate 11 belong to this arrangement. Or this curvilinear figure may be more easily explained by placing two equilateral triangles on each side of a common base, and describing a circle from each of the four vertices, with radius equal to half the side of the triangle (see *B*, Plate 1). But this form of the ogee is not invariable, because it may be, and is frequently much elongated, by substituting isosceles triangles in the place of equilateral triangles, according to the following construction (see Figures *A* and *B*, on Plate 3). Bisect the equal sides of an isosceles triangle, produce the base both ways, draw through the vertex a line parallel to the base, then bisect each half side by perpendiculars cutting the produced base or the line parallel to the base. From the points of intersection *b* or *d* describe arcs of circles *(a c)* through the angular or middle points of the sides.

The interminable variations of which this curve is capable, are doubtless that form known to artists as the "line of beauty," and which is represented as such by our great painter Hogarth. Its manifold combinations form the staple of all flowing tracery, because it is not at all necessary that the upper and lower limbs of the curve should be segments of circles having equal radius. From this elementary principle have resulted all the beautiful compositions of the decorated and flamboyant styles of Gothic architecture.

3. The division of the panel into rectangular parallelograms, see numbers 2 and 4 on Plate 2.

4. Panels having their origin in the subdivision of a given circle into a number of sectors. This class embraces numbers 1 and 2 on Plate 12, and Plates 13 to 20 inclusive. Some of the specimens in this subdivision are extremely curious, and perhaps are without their parallel in any other examples, but the architect and antiquary attach the principal value to those formed upon the square and the triangle, because they not only form the most elegant examples, but verify a principle, since they are based upon the same analytical elements as examples in various other places. Some indeed are of the same pattern, or nearly so, as examples in the Author's " Geometric Paneling of Carlisle Cathedral"; for instance, compare numbers 1, 3, 4 on Plate 1, and No. 3 on Plate 2, with Plates 2, 3, and 6 of the work just named.

DESCRIPTION OF THE PLATES.

⁎ The numbers attached to the ribs of the title plate correspond to those upon each particular illustration.

Plate 1, No. 1.—Consists of the mere introduction of a circle within a square, and within this circle a quatrefoil, or four equal circles inscribed within one (see *a a*). The small circular knobs, introduced within the space lying between the four circles in mutual contact, are unusual in this class of design.

Plate 1, No. 2.—Equally simple as the former, being quatrefoils formed within the diagonals of a given number of equal squares. The quatrefoil varies from the preceding, by being formed of semicircles whose diameter is equal to the side of the square (see *b*).

Plate 1, No. 3.—The panel is divided thus: the width into six and the height into seven parts. Draw the semicircles *c*, whose radius is one part of the width, and then removing the centres to the point of contact of the semicircles *c c*, draw the inverted semicircles *d d*. For the ogee which runs through the framework thus formed, bisect one part of the width, represented by the line *e*, and let the arc of a circle, with its centre on the line *f*, cut the intersections *g g g*.

Plate 1, No. 4.—This example is in principle the same as the preceding, the difference being only in a change of the number of parts. It is a singular demonstration of the fact that a very slight difference of detail frequently constitutes another design. Here the introduction of the quatrefoil, instead of the leaf of the last panel, forms the only alteration.

Plate 2.—Numbers 2 and 4 on this plate have the whole of the divisional lines retained on the completed panel. Both have the same transverse lines (*a*), and the only difference of design is the trefoil heads of Number 2, consequent upon the enlargement of the pattern.

Number 1 retains the alternate perpendicular divisional lines in the shape of a stem, from which the tracery branches. The height and the width are divided into six parts respectively, and each part of the height is again subdivided into three. From 2 2 on the line *b* draw the semicircles *a a*. The framework is completed by the repetition of these, and the introduction of a circle touching the semicircles *a a* and the perpendicular *b*. The examples in Plates 7, 8, are also formed by the tracery springing from stems.

Number 3 on this plate is described with plate 11.

Plate 3.—Draw the square *a*, then the inscribed square *b*, also the diagonals *c c*. The intersecting of these lines with the sides of the inscribed square are the centres of the circles *d*. At *e* is the tracery rib of the full size.

Plate 4 has the same ground-work as the last, but the result is quite different, owing to the doubling of the diagonal ribs and the introduction of foliage, which really gives it the appearance of being referable to a much earlier date than these designs generally. Divide the diagonal into eighteen parts. The interstices between parts 8 and 10 subdivided into three are the substance of the two ribs and the space between these latter. The middle circle (*c*) is of the same radius as the angular concentric circle *b*, the radius of the latter depending upon the width of the rib—*d d*, an arc connecting the diagonal ribs, is part of the circumference of a circle which cuts the intersections *d d* and touches the diagonals of the square at *e e*—*f*, is a full size section of the rib, which has a groove or division in the centre of its face. One-half of the rib thus divided passes under, and the other half over the portions with which it comes in contact. The representation of bolts at the angles of the square renders this specimen of interpenetration exceedingly singular.

Plate 5.—Divide the diagonal of one of the squares into six parts. The curves *a* 2 *a* and *a* 4 *a* are portions of a circle passing through three intersections, two of which are the angular points of the square, the third being at the first diagonal subdivision from the centre. Within the space lying between four of these arcs describe four equal circles (*b*), and within the figure *c* two equal circles in contact with the segmental arcs and each other. In this class of pattern the arc *a* 2 *a* would generally be a quadrant, described from the centre *b*, and the leading figure, instead of being four arcs within a square, would be a circle, which is the case with

Plate 6—which is very nearly allied to the preceding design, although different to the eye. Thus there are the four circles *d*, correspondent to those at *b* in Plate 5, although, for some unknown reason, the circles of Plate 6 are not all of equal radius. The appearance of variation in this design is caused by the retention of the diagonal lines, and the use of four circles *e e* (instead of two, as in the preceding plate), in the space bounded by the arcs *b c*. The facility of producing a different design upon the same ground-work is again exemplified at *f* on the diagram.

Plate 7 has been referred to in the description of Plate 2, as having its tracery springing from a stem, which in this instance would appear on the perpendiculars of every fourth square necessarily used in projecting the design. On each side of the line (or stem) *g*, describe the circles *a a*. Bisect the side of the square on the line *b*, and *c c* will be the centres of the arcs *d d*, touching the divisional line *h—e f* are two equal circles contained within the arcs *d d* and the perpendicular *g*, and *i* is a circle touching *e f*, and the intersection *k*.

Plate 8.—Here the circle *a* branching from the central stem is the same figure as *a* in Plate 7; but, from the circle being of larger dimensions, more detail is introduced within it. After forming the principal circles, draw the perpendicular *g*, at a distance equal to half the side of one square from *f*. Then *b* is an arc having its centre upon the intersection of this perpendicular with the base line. Its radius is the extent of the line *o*. The arc *c* is an inverted repetition of *b*, and *d* is also an arc of the same radius, having its centre on the line 1, and its circumference cutting the intersection of the circle *a* and the arc *c* at *p*. From the arc *c* as a centre draw the circle *i*, touching the arcs *b d*. Then *k k* are two equal circles between the arcs *b d*, and the circle *l* passing through their point of contact is of the same radius as the circle *i*.

Plate 9.—Draw the diagonals *b b*, and the bisecting lines of the square *c c*. Then describe the arcs *e e*, and from the point where these intersect the line *c*, at *f* for instance, describe similar arcs touching the sides of the square *a*. Join the extremities of the common chords *k* and *l* by the lines *m m*, and the intersection of the chords by the angular points of an equilateral triangle (*g h h*), having its vertex at *g*, are the centres of the arcs *i i*. The four equal circles within the arcs *i i* are determined as follows :—Taking the portion of the chord *k* intercepted between the lines *g h*, as a common base, describe an opposite equilateral triangle. In these two triangles describe two equal circles, and two others of equal radius touching the last-named circles and the arcs *i i*, between which they lie.

Plate 10.—Although inferior in elegance to many of the others is a remarkable specimen, because it is the only one in which the principal guiding line, that constitutes the basis of the linear developement of the design, fails to be visible in the tracery; we allude to the circle *a* inscribed within the square *d*. Having drawn the diagonals *b b*, bisect the four radii, which consist of equal parts of the diagonals, and with these points of bisection as centres describe the four equal circles *c c c c*. The formation of the tracery at the angular points of the main figure is guided by three equal circles, two of which touch the sides of the square *a a* and the circles *c c*. The third has its centre on the line *b*.

Though the result of this design is perhaps unsatisfactory, the sketch of one quarter (see page 2), which is based on the main lines just described, proves that the foundation is not objectionable, for the introduction of a little accessory ornament, in which the original, excepting its central portion, is deficient, produces a model much more pleasing to the eye.

Plate 11.—Although at first sight it may not be obvious, this design is based upon the same primary curvilinear form, namely, the ogee, which is groundwork of numbers 3 and 4 on Plate 1. From the circles *a a*, draw the lines 1 1, to the centres *b b* at the base of the panel, and from *c c* the corresponding lines 2 2 to the centres *d d*. These lines are the stems of the elongated trefoils marked 3 on the panel. Form the dotted circle *f*, and divide it into six equal sectors, letting two of the points of division be on the line *b d*. Draw the lines through the adjacent divisions, and these are the stems of the horizontal trefoils which complete the panel. The trefoil heads are all formed by hand, which circumstance considerably mars the effect, which this design would have had, if they had been geometrically drawn.

Plate 12.—This illustration does not belong to the paneling represented in the title plate, being a compartment of the very interesting ancient parish chest of Brancepeth; yet its circular panels bear much upon our subject, and from their simplicity form a very appropriate introduction to the portion yet remaining undescribed, composed, as it is, entirely of designs based upon the subdivision of a leading or primary circle. The chest (of which a view may be seen in Surtees's Durham) has six compartments similar in general design, but varying in the circular panels, and necessarily where the grotesque forms in the spandrils are introduced.

The panel numbered 1 consists of quatrefoils. The diameter of the circle is divided into three equal parts. The diagram No. 2 exhibits the panel represented in the elevation of the compartment. About the circle describe a square and draw its diagonals $a\,a$. Let each side of the square be divided into four equal parts, and describe the four circles b, equal in diameter to one of these parts. The tangents $c\,c$ drawn respectively parallel to the diagonals complete the diagram.

No. 3 consists of six equilateral triangles within a given circle and touching its circumference, being the number produced by the intersection of two equal equilateral triangles, as in the diagram. From the centres a strike the arcs b, and within each triangle place a trefoil. The central hexagon is filled by a circle inclosing a quatrefoil.

No. 4.— Within the circle a, and cutting its centre, draw the lines $b\,b\,b$, from the angular points of a hexagon. Divide the horizontal diameter into six parts, and from parts 2 and 4 draw the lines $a\,a$ parallel to b. These form the width of the hexagonal cross with trefoil heads. At B is a full-sized section of the rib.

Plate 13.—This design appears to have resulted from the stellated model depicted at one corner of the panel—a model, we were wont to describe in the following manner, viz., by taking any point (c) in the circle a and drawing an arc $b\,b$ with the same radius,—then from the points where this intersects the circumference, drawing similar and equal arcs which form the segmental rays— of a thickness (e) thus determined. But the construction of the example under consideration is different, for each arc only extends to the centre of the given circle, and each ray has a distinct and separate centre lying within the circle. The width of the radiating branch is consequently increased. The centres of the curves are, in fact, upon the sides of two equal intersecting equilateral triangles, within the circle. Divide the radius of the circle (as in the figure) into six equal parts and from each vertex of the triangles with radius equal to one of these parts cut the sides in two points, as at 7 7. These points are the centres of the arcs which form the stellar rays.

Plate 14.—The outer annulus of this design is the mere sectorial division of a circle into 48 parts. Place in each sector a semicircle (a) touching the intercepted arc and the radii. Two arcs e and f from the centres b and d on the circumference of the outer circle, form the internal pointed terminations, and the intersection of these arcs also fixes the radius of the inner concentric circle, in which the number of divisions is reduced to sixteen.

Plate 15—In principle is the same as the preceding. Divide the circle *a* into sixteen sectors, and in each place a semicircle *b b* as in the last example. Describe the concentric circle *c* passing through the centres of the circles *b*. Taking the intersection of this circle with the sixteen sectorial radii as centres describe circles touching every pair of radii, observing that three other radii always interpose between them. The intersection of two of these circles, having their centres at *d d*, gives the inner point or arch of the trefoil at *e*, and also fixes the size of the inner concentric circle.

Plate 16.—Divide the circle into 20 sectorial parts. From the division numbered 1 draw a line to 9, then from 9 to 17, and so on round the figure, always leaving an interval of eight parts until the chords terminate at the starting point (from 15 to 1). Their intersection, for instance of the lines 9 and 11 at *a*, determines the size of the secondary concentric circle which contains eleven trefoil heads, whose size is fixed by the circles *l l*. From the point 7 with radius equal to three circumferential divisions describe the arc *d*, and from the point 3 describe a corresponding arc from 6. Their junction at *f* gives the size of the inner circle. The small diagram at the side of the plate represents the six leaved ornament of the centre. Within the circle describe a hexagon, draw radii to each of the angular points, and upon each radius, and the same side of it describe a semicircle as *b*. The radius of the arc *d*, forming the second side of each leaf, is equal to four-thirds of the preceding.

Plate 17 has the appearance of being complex, but its construction is very simple. Divide the circle into twelve equal sectorial parts. Within the circle *d* draw three equidistant concentric circles indicated respectively *a b c*. Upon each of the sectorial radii and on the same side of it draw a semicircle as *e* and *f*. From the centre *k*, in the circumference of the second circle *c*, describe the arc *g* of equal radius to the semicircles *e f*. Describe the accessory concentric circle *l*, and upon it fix the centre of the arc *h*, touching one of the semicircles *e* and passing through the intersection of the arcs *f* and *g*. This arc is also of the same radius as the preceding. There is another panel, placed next to number 1 on the title plate, which is almost a fac-simile of this. It differs principally in having the six leaved central ornament of the preceding example.

14

Plate 18 bears a close analogy to the last specimen. The circle being divided into sixteen equal sectorial parts, eight of the radii represent the central ribs of the pattern. Describe eight circles touching every pair of radii that have three other radii lying between them, as for instance the circle touching the radii 1 and 5, the arc *a* being only necessary to the design. Describe the circle *b* passing through the centres of the above-named eight, and from the centre *f* on the radius marked 14 describe the arc cutting the radius 11. Draw another accessory equidistant circle *d*, and upon it fix the centre of the arc *e*, touching two of the eight circles first named.

Plate 19.—This singular panel has its origin in the division of a circle into thirty-four equal sectors, and its radius into five, marked respectively *a b c d e*. From the point 1 on the circle *c* draw a line through the intersection 7 to the circumference of the outer circle, and then from point 2 draw a corresponding line through the intersection 8. The repetition of this process upon the whole number of thirty-four lines completes the figure in the outer ring. The inner lines, which are sixteen in number, run exactly in an opposite direction to the preceding. Draw a line from 14 to 27, then from 16 to 29, and so on, until the number is completed. The central figure made by the intersection of these chords determines the size of the circle *k*.

Plate 20.—Divide the breadth of the panel into five equal parts and draw the bisecting perpendicular. Then from the point 2 at the top of the panel, with distance equal to four-fifths of the whole width, cut the divisional line 4 in *A*, which is the centre of the arc 1. The inverted arcs 4 4 are of the same radius. Draw the horizontal bisecting line *C*, then the bisecting line 2 5 between the arcs 1 4. Taking their point of intersection as the centre of the figure, inscribe within each half the circles *a a*, touching the intersection and the arcs 1 4. From the centres of the arcs 4 4, marked *B*, draw the lines *B D E*. Then from *D D* and *E* describe the equal circles 5, 6, 7. Then describe the circle *b* touching the circles 5 6, the arc 4, and the perpendicular 5 *D*. The circumference of the small circle *c* passes through the centre of the circle *b*, and the arcs *d d* are repetitions of the circles 5 6.

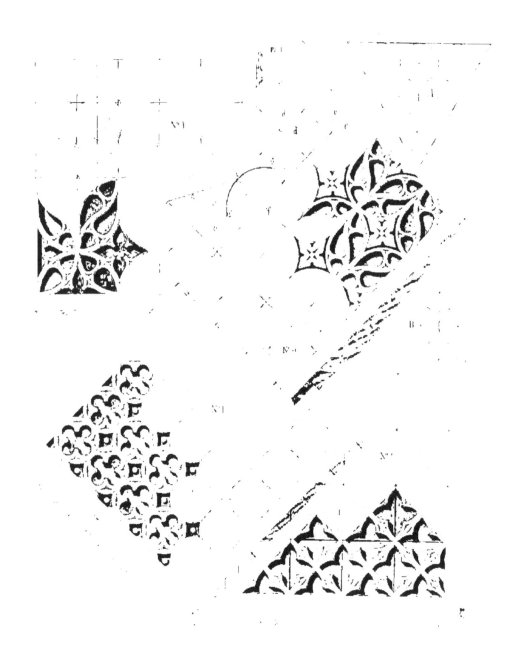

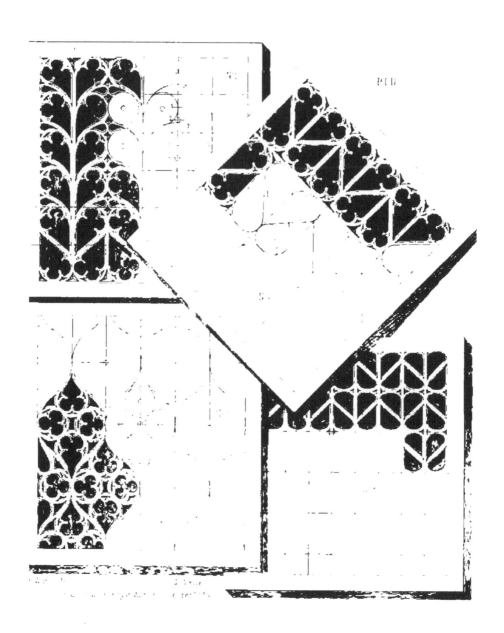

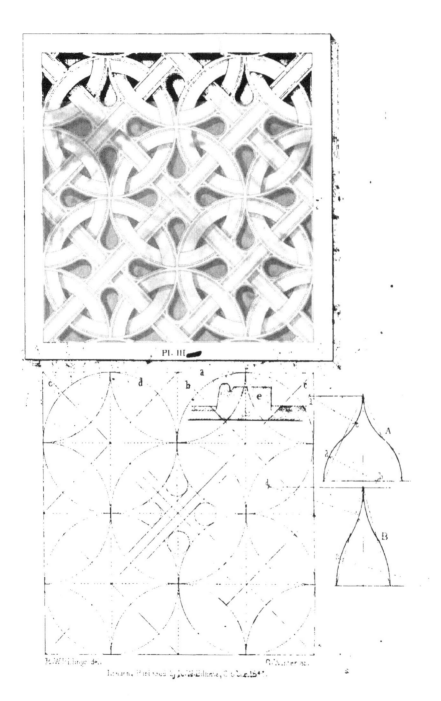

Pl. III

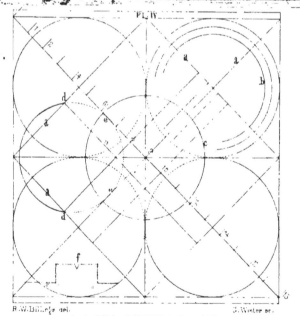

PL. IV.

R.W.Billings del.

J.Winter sc.

London, Published by R.W.Billings, October 1844.

Pl. V

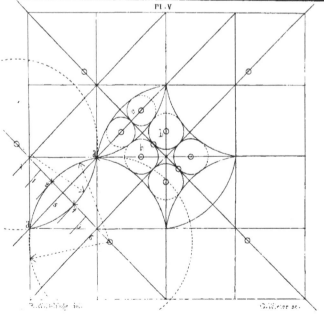

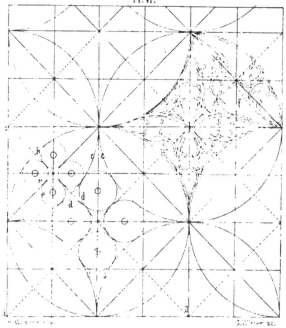

Pl. VI.

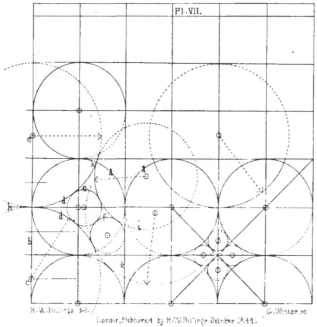

Pl. VII.

R. W. Billings del.

C. Winter sc.

London, Published by R. W. Billings October 1844.

Pl. VIII.

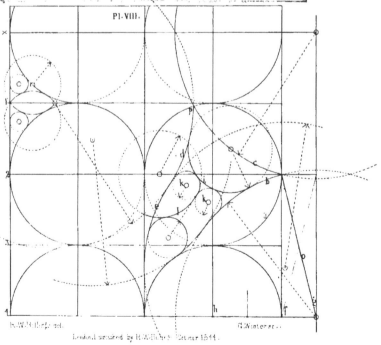

R.W.B... del.   G. Winter sc...

London, published by R.W.Billings, October 1844.

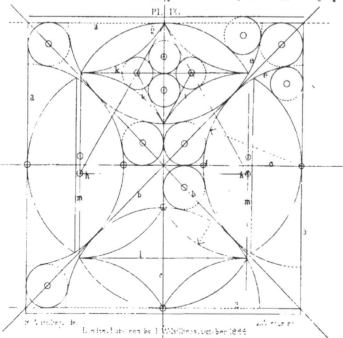

Pl. IX.

London, Published by J. Williams, October 1844

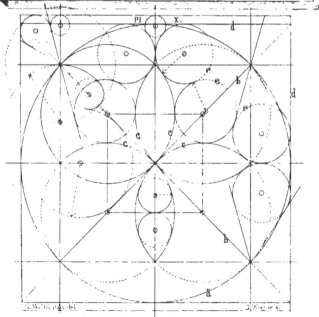

London, Published by E.& F.N. Spon, October 1864.

Pl. XI

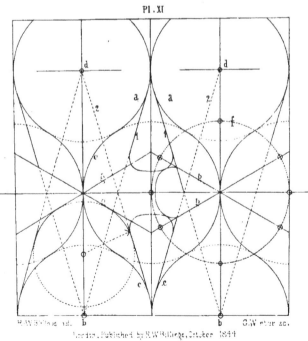

R.W.Billings del.   G.W. etur sc.

London, Published by R.W.Billings, October 1844

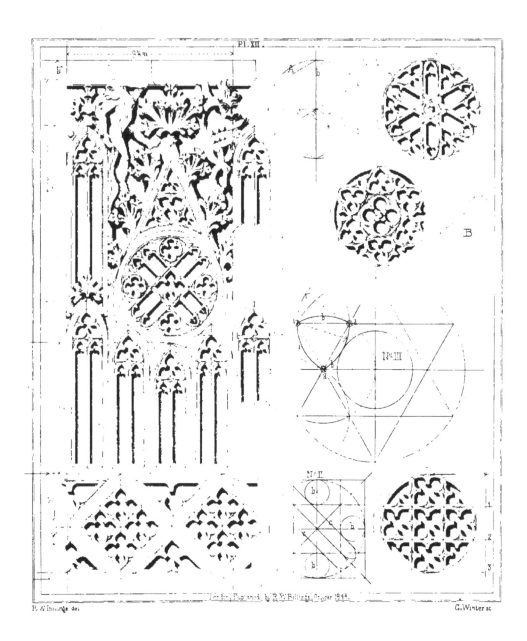

Pl. XII.

A.

B.

N.º III

N.º II

London, Published by R. W. Billings, August 1844.

R. W. Billings del.

G. Winter sc.

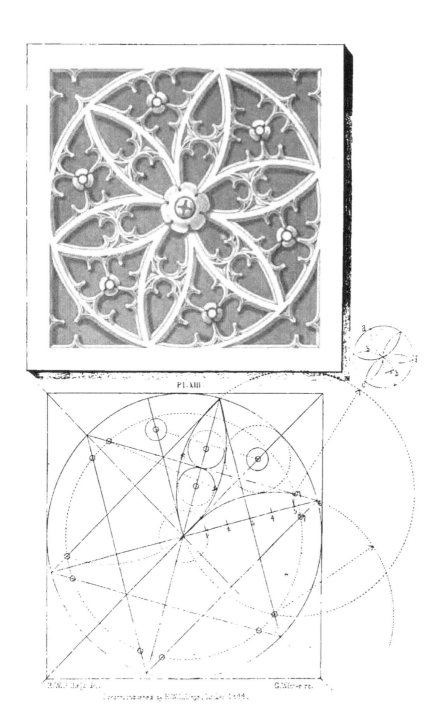

PL. XIII.

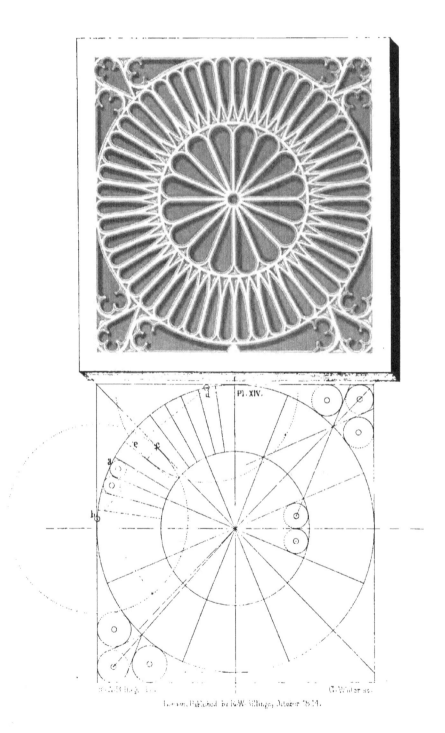

Pl. XIV.

London, Published by R.W. Billings, October 1844.

Pl. XV.

R W Billings del.

London Published by P.W.P. Hugh October 1841

G Winter sc.

Pl. XVI.

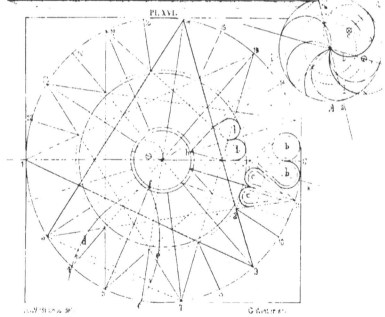

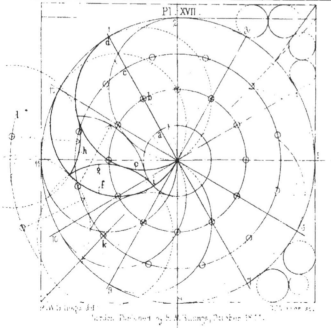

Pl. XVII.

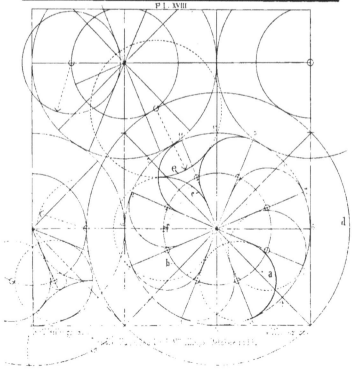

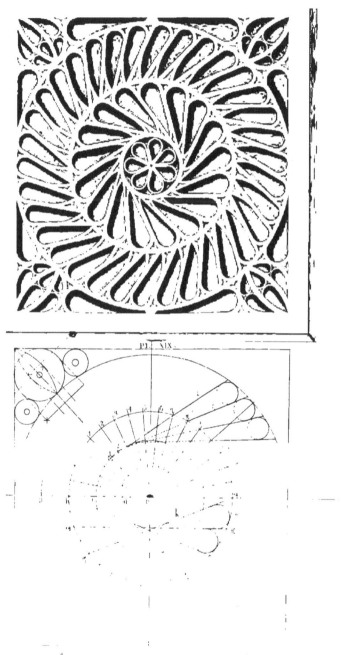

PL. XIX.

London, published by ...

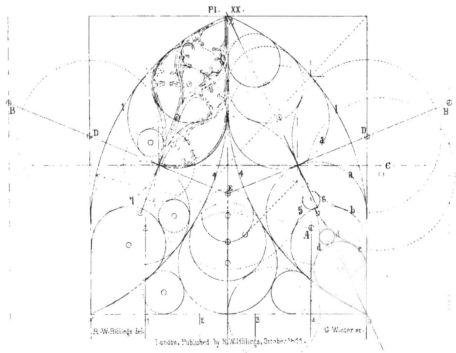

R.W.Billings del.

London, Published by R.W.Billings, October 1844.

G Winter sc.

NOW PUBLISHED, PARTS I. TO VIII., OF THE

ARCHITECTURAL ANTIQUITIES OF THE COUNTY OF DURHAM,

BY

ROBERT WILLIAM BILLINGS,

AUTHOR OF THE ILLUSTRATIONS OF DURHAM CATHEDRAL.

THE ENGRAVINGS BY J. H. LE KEUX AND GEORGE WINTER.

This Work will contain Sixty Engravings on Steel, of the principal Churches, Castles, and other Antiquities, from Drawings made on the spot. These will be accompanied by Descriptive Accounts of each.

It will be Published (at intervals of two months) in Fifteen Parts, each with Four Plates at Two Shillings in Medium Quarto ; and Four Shillings in Imperial Quarto with Proofs of the Plates on India Paper. The Letter-press Description will be delivered gratis with the concluding Part.

The whole expense will be Thirty Shillings for the Medium Quarto, and Three Pounds for the Proofs.

It will only be necessary to mention a few of the principal Subjects to be Illustrated, in order to shew that a very interesting Volume may be formed, and no pains will be spared in effecting this object. Among the

ECCLESIASTICAL EDIFICES

Those of the CATHEDRAL, LINDISFARNE, FINCHALE, BRANCEPETH, CHESTER-LE-STREET, DARLING-TON, HARTLEPOOL, HOUGHTON-LE-SPRING, and STAINDROP, may be named ; and the

CASTELLATED SPECIMENS

Will include DURHAM, BRANCEPETH, BARNARDCASTLE, LUMLEY, RABY, HYLTON, &c.

LONDON : PUBLISHED BY T. AND W. BOONE, 29, NEW BOND STREET,
FOR
GEORGE ANDREWS, SADDLER STREET, DURHAM ; AND
ROBERT WILLIAM BILLINGS.

WORKS BY THE SAME AUTHOR.

Printed uniformly with Pugin's and Britton's Works,

ARCHITECTURAL ILLUSTRATIONS OF DURHAM CATHEDRAL,

CONTAINING SEVENTY-FIVE ENGRAVINGS AND LETTER-PRESS DESCRIPTIONS.

Price Five Guineas Medium Quarto ; Seven Guineas and a Half Imperial Quarto.

⁎⁎ The total numbers printed of this work, agreeably to the terms of the original Prospectus, were 125 Large Paper, and 600 Small Paper copies. Impressions of the destroyed Plates may be seen at the Publishers.

ARCHITECTURAL ILLUSTRATIONS AND DESCRIPTION OF CARLISLE
CATHEDRAL,

CONTAINING FORTY-FIVE ENGRAVINGS, THREE WOOD-CUTS, AND TWELVE SHEETS OF LETTER-PRESS.

Price Three Guineas Medium Quarto ; Four Guineas and a Half Imperial Quarto.

*The Plans, Elevations, and Sections of both Durham and Carlisle are to the same Scale, and form the first parallel
ever published of the English Cathedral.*

ILLUSTRATIONS OF GOTHIC GEOMETRIC PANELING FROM THE CATHEDRAL
CHURCH OF CARLISLE,

CONTAINING TWENTY PLATES, WITH DESCRIPTIONS OF THE SYSTEM UPON WHICH THE PANELS ARE
COMPOSED.

*It will be found to convey to the Architectural Student and to the Workman, a sure means of reproducing the
forms displayed in the beautiful examples represented ; and a careful examination of their construction will shew the
easy manner in which, by a different arrangement of the same forms, other combinations may be produced. These
principles may be successfully applied by the Designer, wheresoever ornamental tracery can be introduced.*

Price—Medium Quarto, Fifteen Shillings ; Imperial Quarto, Twenty-four Shillings.

Also, in continuation of the subject of the above Publication,

ILLUSTRATIONS OF GEOMETRIC TRACERY FROM THE CHURCH OF BRANCEPETH,
NEAR DURHAM.

Price Twelve Shillings in Medium Quarto ; and One Guinea Imperial Quarto.

AN ATTEMPT TO DEFINE THE GEOMETRICAL PROJECTION OF GOTHIC
ARCHITECTURE,

AS EXEMPLIFIED BY THE CATHEDRALS OF CARLISLE AND WORCESTER.

ILLUSTRATED BY FIVE PLATES.

Price Five Shillings in Medium Quarto ; and Ten Shillings and Sixpence Imperial Quarto, sewed.

ARCHITECTURAL ILLUSTRATIONS AND DESCRIPTION OF THE TEMPLE
CHURCH, LONDON.

This Work contains Thirty-one PLATES, illustrative of the most interesting Examples of the Lancet,
or first Pointed Architecture, in this country, wholly Drawn and Engraved by the Author.

Price Two Guineas Medium Quarto ; Three Guineas Imperial Quarto.

The Plates of this Work are destroyed, and very few Copies remain for sale.

ARCHITECTURAL ILLUSTRATIONS OF KETTERING CHURCH,
NORTHAMPTONSHIRE,

WITH TWENTY PLATES ENGRAVED BY G. WINTER, AND TWO SHEETS OF LETTER-PRESS.

Price Ten Shillings and Sixpence Medium Quarto ; and Twenty-one Shillings Imperial Quarto,
with Proofs on India Paper.

LONDON : PUBLISHED BY T. AND W. BOONE, 29, NEW BOND STREET.

Lightning Source UK Ltd.
Milton Keynes UK
UKOW07f1134110515

251263UK00001B/106/P